Weather Patterns

Monica Hughes

D0316016

www.heinemann.co.uk/library

Visit our website to find out more information about **Heinemann Library** books.

To order:
☎ Phone 44 (0) 1865 888066
🖨 Send a fax to 44 (0) 1865 314091
💻 Visit the Heinemann Bookshop at www.heinemann.co.uk/library to browse our catalogue and order online.

First published in Great Britain by Heinemann Library, Halley Court, Jordan Hill, Oxford OX2 8EJ, part of Harcourt Education. Heinemann is a registered trademark of Harcourt Education Ltd.

© Harcourt Education Ltd 2004.
First published in paperback in 2005.
The moral right of the proprietor has been asserted.

All rights reserved. No part of this publication may be reproduced, stored in a retrieval system, or transmitted in any form or by any means, electronic, mechanical, photocopying, recording, or otherwise, without either the prior written permission of the Publishers or a licence permitting restricted copying in the United Kingdom issued by the Copyright Licensing Agency Ltd, 90 Tottenham Court Road, London W1T 4LP (www.cla.co.uk).

Editorial: Jilly Attwood, Kate Bellamy
Design: Jo Hinton-Malivoire
Picture research: Ginny Stroud-Lewis, Ruth Blair
Production: Séverine Ribierre

Originated by Ambassador Litho Ltd
Printed and bound in China by South China Printing Company

ISBN 0 431 11395 5 (hardback)
08 07 06 05 04
10 9 8 7 6 5 4 3 2 1

ISBN 0 431 11401 3 (paperback)
09 08 07 06 05
10 9 8 7 6 5 4 3 2 1

British Library Cataloguing in Publication Data
Hughes, Monica
Weather Patterns - (Nature's Patterns)
551.6
A full catalogue record for this book is available from the British Library.

Acknowledgements
The Publishers would like to thank the following for permission to reproduce photographs: Alamy p. **21**; Corbis pp. **4**, **5**, **6**, **13**, **18**, **19**, **22**; Corbis pp. **29** (Mike Chew), **14** (Mark A Johnson), **24** (Ray Juno), **8** (Richard Klune), **25** (Gunter Marx), **20** (Charles O'Rear), **16** (Time Page), **27** (Galen Rowell), **15** (royalty free); Getty Images p. **17**; Getty Images p. **23** (Image Bank); Corbis pp. **4**, **5**, **6**, **13**, **18**, **19**, **22**; Noaa p. **28**; Oxford Scientific Films p. **26**.

Cover photograph of rainbow over Mauritius is reproduced with permission of Corbis.

Our thanks to David Lewin for his assistance in the preparation of this book.

Every effort has been made to contact copyright holders of any material reproduced in this book. Any omissions will be rectified in subsequent printings if notice is given to the Publishers.

The paper used to print this book comes from sustainable resources.

NEWCASTLE UPON TYNE CITY LIBRARIES	
C4 301183 OO XO	
Askews	Jun-2005
J551.6	£6.25

Contents

Words appearing in the text in bold, **like this**, are explained in the Glossary.

 Find out more about Nature's Patterns at www.heinemannexplore.co.uk

Nature's patterns

Nature is always changing. Many of the changes follow a **pattern**. This means that they happen over and over again.

In some storms, there is a pattern of lightening and thunder.

The pattern of sun and rain creates a rainbow.

There are patterns in the weather a place has. Some weather patterns have a clear beginning and end. There are different weather patterns around the world.

A pattern every day

There is a **temperature pattern** that happens every day. It is cool in the early morning, warmer towards **midday** and coldest at night.

The temperature pattern happens because the Earth is always turning. Places are warm when they face the Sun. They get cooler as they turn away from the Sun.

A pattern every year

Most places also have a yearly weather **pattern**. They have the same weather at the same time each year. The different times are called seasons.

The weather is warmest in the summer.

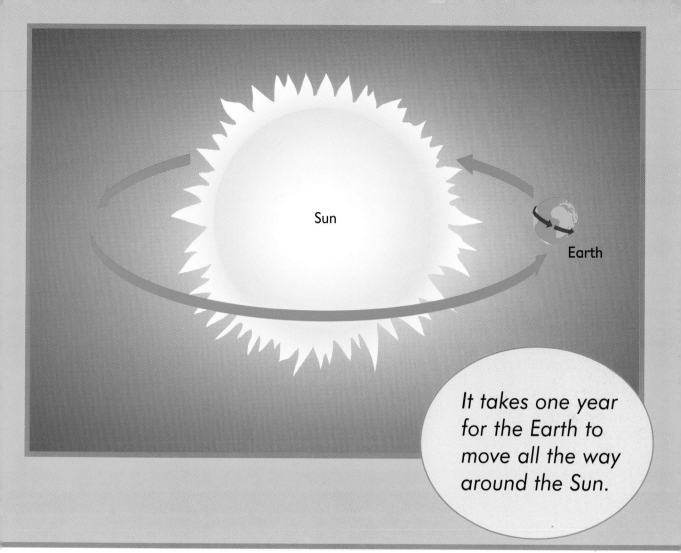

It takes one year for the Earth to move all the way around the Sun.

Yearly weather patterns happen because the Earth moves around the Sun. As the Earth moves, some parts are nearest the Sun. Some parts are further away.

Climate patterns

The weather **pattern** that a place has is called its **climate**. The climate is linked to heat from the Sun. The heat reaches the Earth in the Sun's **rays**.

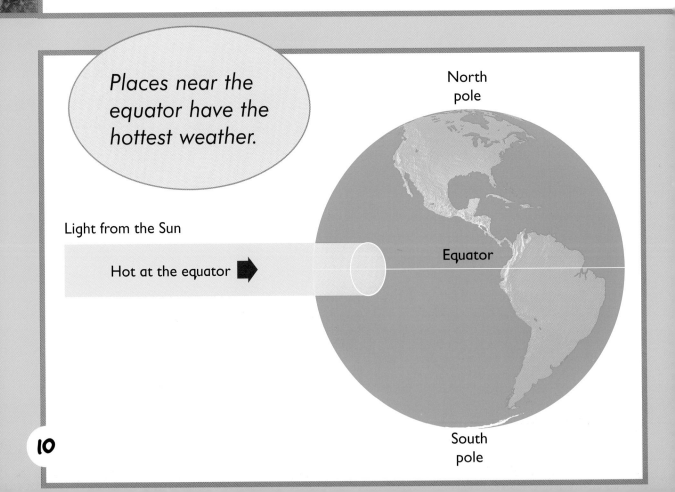

Places near the equator have the hottest weather.

North pole

Light from the Sun

Hot at the equator ➡

Equator

South pole

Around the **equator** it is hot all year. At the equator the Sun's rays hit the Earth straight on. Sun rays are strongest when they travel straight to Earth.

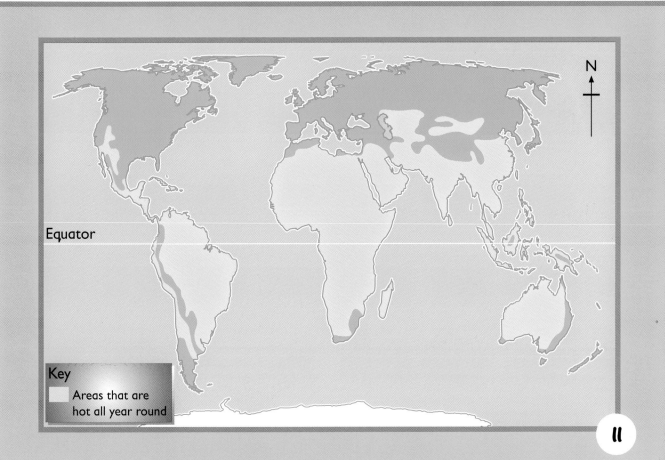

Equator

Key
Areas that are hot all year round

Different climate patterns

Climate patterns are different around the world. Away from the **equator** the Sun's **rays** don't hit the Earth straight on. They hit the Earth at an **angle**.

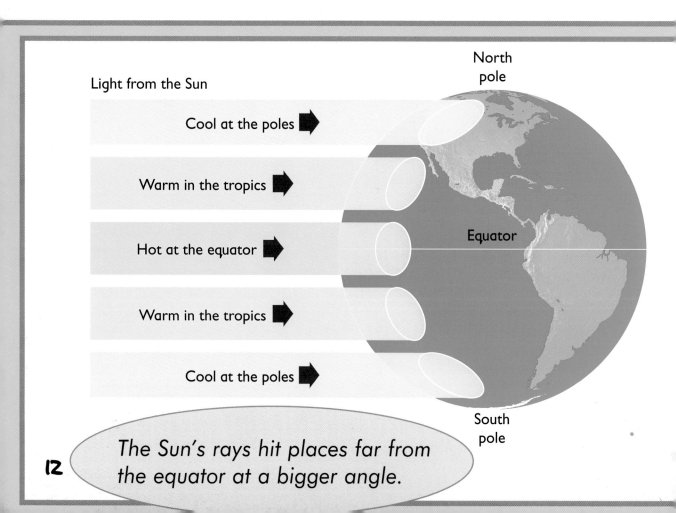

Light from the Sun

Cool at the poles

Warm in the tropics

Hot at the equator

Warm in the tropics

Cool at the poles

North pole

Equator

South pole

The Sun's rays hit places far from the equator at a bigger angle.

When the Sun's rays hit the Earth at an angle they cover a wider area. The heat is less strong.

At the Poles the Sun's rays fall at a greater angle. These places are cold all year round.

Hot and wet

Places closest to the **equator** do not have different seasons. These areas have a **tropical climate**. It is hot and wet all year round.

The hot wet climate of the rainforest is good for plants.

Some rainforests have thunderstorms and heavy rain every afternoon.

Rainforests have a tropical climate. They have the same **pattern** every day. The night is coolest and the mornings are hot and sunny. During the day, clouds form and it rains in the afternoon.

Dry and wet

Some places with a **tropical climate** are hot all year but have two different seasons. Half of the year it is dry. Half of the year it is wet.

Storm clouds begin to gather at the start of the wet season.

The wet season can begin suddenly with very heavy rain and strong winds. This rain and wind is called a **monsoon**.

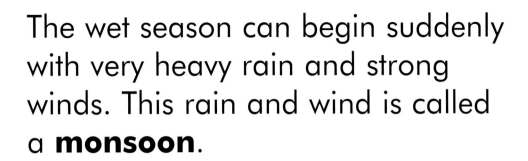

Monsoon rains often cause flooding.

Hot and dry

Desert areas around the **equator** are hot and dry. They also have a daily **pattern** of very cold nights and long hot days.

A desert's wet season may be short if there is very little rain. If there is too little rain, the desert has a **drought**. A drought can last for months or years.

When there is no rain the ground dries and cracks.

Seasonal patterns

Some parts of the world have four different seasons. Spring is warm. Summer is hot and sunny. There is often very little rain.

Warm climates are good for growing fruit.

It rains in winter but is not very cold.

Autumn is cool but winter is **mild**. Winter has more rain than summer but not much frost or snow. This is called a warm **temperate climate**.

Different seasonal patterns

In other places each season has its own very different **pattern** of weather. Autumn is cool and wet. Winter is long and very cold with frost or snow.

Special lorries have to clear snow from the road in winter.

Lambs are born in the spring time.

Spring and summer have higher **temperatures** and less rain than autumn and winter. Summer can be hot but the weather changes often.

More seasonal patterns

Places far from the **equator** have a colder **climate**. They have a short spring and autumn. The summers are also short but can be hot.

Summer only lasts for about two months in cold climates.

The winters are long and very cold in places far from the equator. The days are much shorter than in the summer.

The winter is so cold that lakes and seas freeze over.

Polar patterns

The North Pole and the South Pole are furthest from the **equator**. Summer is very cold. The Sun is low in the sky. The ground stays frozen all year.

The North Pole is in the Arctic and the South Pole is in the Antarctic.

The winters in the North and South pole are very long and very cold. Strong winds are common and these cause snow storms.

There is hardly any daylight in winter.

What will the weather be like?

Knowing the weather **pattern** in an area helps to **predict** what the weather will be. People know what clothes to wear and when to expect rain.

Snow

Rain

AM Snow

Snow

Snow

Heavy Snow Possible

Snow

Rain

Rain

Snow

People who predict the weather use a map to show us what they think the weather will be.

Predicting the weather helps people know where to go for winter sports.

People know where there will be snow if they want to ski. Or where it will be hot if they want to swim in the sea.

Look for a pattern

Record the **temperature** every hour over two or three days. Use the same place every day. Find somewhere outside but away from direct sunlight.

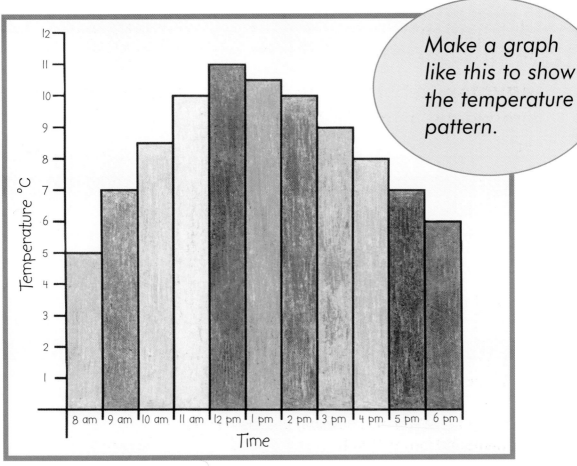

Make a graph like this to show the temperature pattern.

Find out more about Nature's Patterns at www.heinemannexplore.co.uk

Glossary

angle the way something slopes or slants

climate usual weather pattern of an area

desert dry sandy area with little rain

drought time when there is no rain

equator imaginary line around the middle of the earth

midday the middle of the day at 12 o'clock

monsoon season of heavy rain

pattern something that happens over and over again

predict say what will happen in the future

rays straight lines of sunlight

temperature how hot or cold it is

tropical a very hot and rainy area

More books to read

Watching the Weather: Clouds, Elisabeth Miles (Heinemann Library, 2004)

Watching the Weather: Sunshine, Elisabeth Miles (Heinemann Library, 2004)

Index